SCHOLASTIC

Now I Know My

SIGHT WORDS

Learning Mats

50+ Double-Sided Activity Sheets That Help Children
Read, Write, and Learn More Than 100 High-Frequency Words

Lucia Kemp Henry

New York • Toronto • London • Auckland • Sydney
Mexico City • New Delhi • Hong Kong • Buenos Aires

Teaching
Resources

Edited by Immacula A. Rhodes
Cover design by Scott Davis
Interior illustrations by Lucia Kemp Henry
Interior design by Holly Grundon

ISBN: 978-0-545-39702-5

8 9 10   40   19

Contents

About This Book 5

Dolch Basic Sight Word Vocabulary List 7

Meeting the Standards 8

Learning Mats

Mat	Skill	Mat	Skill
1	Sight Word: *all*	24	Sight Word: *from*
2	Sight Word: *am*	25	Sight Word: *funny*
3	Sight Word: *and*	26	Sight Word: *gave*
4	Sight Word: *are*	27	Sight Word: *get*
5	Sight Word: *as*	28	Sight Word: *go*
6	Sight Word: *ask*	29	Sight Word: *goes*
7	Sight Word: *ate*	30	Sight Word: *good*
8	Sight Word: *away*	31	Sight Word: *had*
9	Sight Word: *be*	32	Sight Word: *have*
10	Sight Word: *big*	33	Sight Word: *he*
11	Sight Word: *blue*	34	Sight Word: *help*
12	Sight Word: *but*	35	Sight Word: *her*
13	Sight Word: *by*	36	Sight Word: *here*
14	Sight Word: *came*	37	Sight Word: *him*
15	Sight Word: *come*	38	Sight Word: *his*
16	Sight Word: *did*	39	Sight Word: *how*
17	Sight Word: *do*	40	Sight Word: *into*
18	Sight Word: *does*	41	Sight Word: *is*
19	Sight Word: *down*	42	Sight Word: *jump*
20	Sight Word: *eat*	43	Sight Word: *just*
21	Sight Word: *find*	44	Sight Word: *like*
22	Sight Word: *for*	45	Sight Word: *little*
23	Sight Word: *found*	46	Sight Word: *look*

Learning Mats (continued)

Mat	Skill	Mat	Skill
47	Sight Word: *make*	76	Sight Word: *soon*
48	Sight Word: *many*	77	Sight Word: *that*
49	Sight Word: *my*	78	Sight Word: *the*
50	Sight Word: *new*	79	Sight Word: *their*
51	Sight Word: *no*	80	Sight Word: *them*
52	Sight Word: *not*	81	Sight Word: *then*
53	Sight Word: *now*	82	Sight Word: *there*
54	Sight Word: *of*	83	Sight Word: *they*
55	Sight Word: *off*	84	Sight Word: *this*
56	Sight Word: *on*	85	Sight Word: *too*
57	Sight Word: *our*	86	Sight Word: *under*
58	Sight Word: *out*	87	Sight Word: *us*
59	Sight Word: *over*	88	Sight Word: *very*
60	Sight Word: *play*	89	Sight Word: *want*
61	Sight Word: *please*	90	Sight Word: *was*
62	Sight Word: *pretty*	91	Sight Word: *well*
63	Sight Word: *put*	92	Sight Word: *went*
64	Sight Word: *read*	93	Sight Word: *were*
65	Sight Word: *red*	94	Sight Word: *what*
66	Sight Word: *ride*	95	Sight Word: *when*
67	Sight Word: *right*	96	Sight Word: *where*
68	Sight Word: *run*	97	Sight Word: *who*
69	Sight Word: *said*	98	Sight Word: *will*
70	Sight Word: *saw*	99	Sight Word: *with*
71	Sight Word: *say*	100	Sight Word: *would*
72	Sight Word: *see*	101	Sight Word: *yellow*
73	Sight Word: *she*	102	Sight Word: *yes*
74	Sight Word: *so*	103	Sight Word: *you*
75	Sight Word: *some*	104	Sight Word: *your*

About This Book

Welcome to *Now I Know My Sight Words Learning Mats*! The double-sided mats in this book provide engaging activities designed to help children master more than 100 high-frequency words. In addition, the systematic format reinforces emerging reading and fine-motor skills while enabling children to work independently.

The interactive, reproducible mats feature appealing art and simple, predictable text that targets 104 words found on the Dolch Basic Sight Word Vocabulary List. (See page 7.) Activities include tracing and writing words to reinforce spelling and working with color-coded pictures to give children practice in word recognition and visual discrimination. The tracing and writing exercises also help develop and strengthen fine-motor skills, as well as reinforce the shape and formation of letters. And, as children read and follow directions to complete each mat, they build important word recognition and comprehension skills. To help meet the learning needs of your students, refer to page 8 to see how activities in this book connect to the Common Core State Standards for Reading (Foundational Skills) and Language.

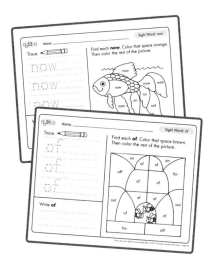

Preparing and using the learning mats is quick and easy! Simply make double-sided copies to use for instruction with the whole class, small groups, student pairs, or individuals. The mats are also ideal for independent work, centers, and homework. You'll find that daily practice with these activities builds recognition of high-frequency words and other early literacy skills. Best of all, children will experience the joy of learning as they develop skills that help them grow into more confident, fluent readers.

What Are Sight Words?

Sight words, or high-frequency words, are the words most commonly encountered in any text. Many of these words may be difficult for children to decode since they do not follow regular rules of spelling. Also, they generally carry little meaning and are not necessarily as easy to define as nouns. Most sight words are known as "function words" rather than "content words." Though they may not appear to carry a clear meaning, these words have a strong impact on the flow and coherence of the text children read.

There are several widely recognized lists of high-frequency words. The words in this book are found on the Dolch Basic Sight Word Vocabulary List, which accounts for more than 50% of the words found in textbooks today.

What's Inside

Each ready-to-go learning mat in this resource targets two specific sight words—one on each side of the mat. The words appear in alphabetical order on the mats. To use, simply decide on the words you want to teach, locate the corresponding mats in the book, and make a double-sided copy of the selected mats. (If you want to teach only one word at a time, copy just the side of the mat for the desired word.) The only materials kids need for the activities are crayons or colored pencils. To use, children read and follow the directions to perform each activity. You'll find the following activities on the mats:

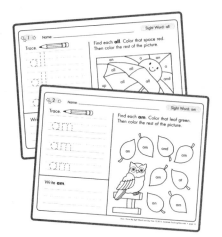

✤ **Trace and Write:** Children trace and write the target word. These exercises reinforce letter formation, build fine-motor skills, and provide word recognition and spelling practice.

✤ **Color-Coded Picture:** This activity reinforces word recognition and visual discrimination skills. Children color each space that contains the target word and then color the rest of the picture as desired. Some of the completed color-coded pictures reveal hidden objects, while others allow children to create colorful objects, creatures, or scenes.

Helpful Tips

The following suggestions will help you and your students get the most out of the learning mats:

● Complete each mat in advance to become familiar with the directions, art, and response for each activity. If desired, laminate your completed copy to use as an answer key. (Or slip the mat into a clear, plastic page protector.) You might bind all of your answer keys into a notebook to keep on hand for children to check their work.

● Use the mats to introduce new concepts, track children's progress in mastering essential skills, and review concepts already covered.

● Prepare the mats for repeated use in learning centers. Simply laminate the double-sided mats and put them in a center along with wipe-off color crayons and paper towels (to use as erasers).

● Compile sets of the learning mats into booklets for children to complete in class or at home. For example, you might staple copies of mats 1–15 between two sheets of construction paper and title the booklet, "My Sight Words from *A* to *C*."

● The mats are also perfect for instant homework assignments. Send the pages home with children to complete. This is an easy way to reinforce skills covered in class as well as to help keep families informed about what their children are learning, what they've mastered, and where they might need some extra guidance.

Dolch Basic Sight Word Vocabulary List

Following are the 220 words that appear on the Dolch Basic Sight Word Vocabulary List.
The words in bold are featured on the learning mats in this book.

Pre-primer	Primer		First Grade	Second Grade	
a	**all**	**under**	after	always	wish
and	**am**	**want**	again	around	work
away	**are**	**was**	an	because	**would**
big	at	**well**	any	been	write
blue	**ate**	**went**	**as**	before	**your**
can	**be**	**what**	**ask**	best	
come	black	white	**by**	both	
down	brown	**who**	could	buy	
find	**but**	**will**	every	call	
for	**came**	**with**	fly	cold	
funny	**did**	**yes**	**from**	**does**	
go	**do**		give	don't	
help	**eat**		giving	fast	
here	four		**had**	first	
I	**get**		has	five	
in	**good**		**her**	**found**	
is	**have**		**him**	**gave**	
it	**he**		**his**	**goes**	
jump	**into**		**how**	green	
little	**like**		**just**	its	
look	must		know	made	
make	**new**		let	**many**	
me	**no**		live	**off**	
my	**now**		may	or	
not	**on**		**of**	pull	
one	**our**		old	**read**	
play	**out**		once	**right**	
red	**please**		open	sing	
run	**pretty**		**over**	sit	
said	ran		**put**	sleep	
see	**ride**		round	tell	
the	**saw**		**some**	**their**	
three	**say**		stop	these	
to	**she**		take	those	
two	**so**		thank	upon	
up	**soon**		**them**	**us**	
we	**that**		**then**	use	
where	**there**		think	**very**	
yellow	**they**		walk	wash	
you	**this**		**were**	which	
	too		**when**	why	

Meeting the Standards

Connections to the Common Core State Standards

The Common Core State Standards Initiative (CCSSI) has outlined learning expectations in English/Language Arts for students at different grade levels. The activities in this book align with the following standards for students in grades K–2. For more information, visit the CCSSI Web site at www.corestandards.org.

Reading Standards: Foundational Skills

Print Concepts

• RF.K.1, RF.1.1. Demonstrate understanding of the organization and basic features of print.

• RF.K.1a. Recognize and name all upper- and lowercase letters of the alphabet.

Phonological Awareness

• RF.K.2, RF.1.2. Demonstrate understanding of spoken words, syllables, and sounds (phonemes).

• RF.K.2b. Count, pronounce, blend, and segment syllables in spoken words.

• RF.1.2 b. Orally produce single-syllable words by blending sounds (phonemes), including consonant blends.

Phonics and Word Recognition

• RF.K.3, RF.1.3, RF.2.3. Know and apply grade-level phonics and word analysis skills in decoding words.

• RF.K.3c. Read common high-frequency words by sight (e.g., *the, of, to, you, she, my, is, are, do, does*).

• RF.1.3a. Know the spelling-sound correspondences for common consonant digraphs (two letters that represent one sound).

• RF.1.3g. Recognize and read grade-appropriate irregularly spelled words.

• RF.2.3f. Recognize and read grade-appropriate irregularly spelled words.

Fluency

• RF.K.4, RF.1.4, RF.2.4. Read with sufficient accuracy and fluency to support comprehension.

• RF.1.4a, RF.2.4a. Read grade-level text with purpose and understanding.

• RF.1.4c, RF.2.4c. Use context to confirm or self-correct word recognition and understanding, rereading as necessary.

Language

Conventions of Standard English

• L.K.1, L.1.1, L.2.1. Demonstrate command of the conventions of standard English grammar and usage when writing or speaking.

• L.K.1a, L.1.1a. Print upper- and lowercase letters.

• L.K.2, L.1.2, L.2.2. Demonstrate command of the conventions of standard English capitalization, punctuation, and spelling when writing.

9 ☆ ☆ ☆

Name: _____

Find each be. Color that space yellow.
Then color the rest of the picture.

be

be

bat

be

be

bun

by

be

Trace.

Write **be.**

Name: _____

Find each **big**. Color that owl brown.
Then color the rest of the picture.

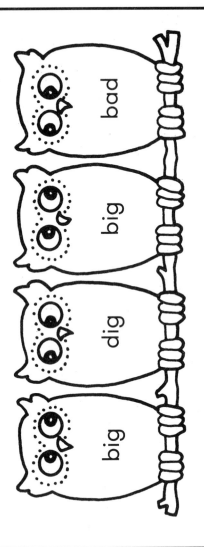

big   dig   big   bad

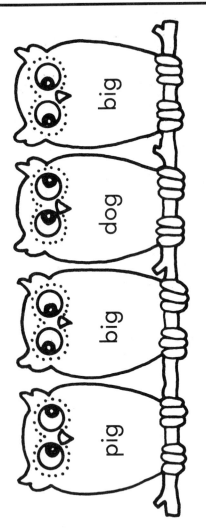

pig   big   dog   big

Trace.

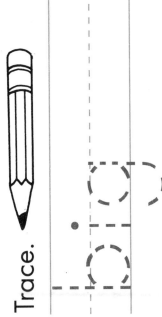

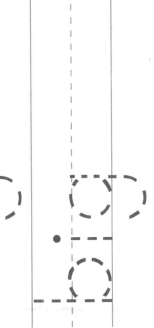

Write **big**.
_____

Name: _____

☆ 11
☆ ☆

Find each **blue**. Color that bird blue.
Then color the rest of the picture.

blue

blow

blue

big

be

by

blue

blue

Trace.

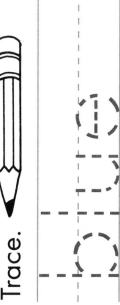

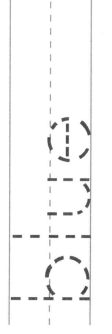

Write **blue**.

☆☆ 12 ☆

Name: _____

Find each **but**. Color that space purple. Then color the rest of the picture.

by	big	be
	but	but
but	did	but
be	but	but
by	but	but
big	did	be

Trace.

b u t

b u t

b u t

Write **but**.

_____

Find each come. Color that mushroom red. Then color the rest of the picture.

come

cone

come

came

came

come

can

come

☆ 15 ☆☆

Name: _____

Trace.

come

come

come

Write **come.** _____

Name: _____

16

Trace.

Write did. _____

Find each **did**. Color that space green.
Then color the rest of the picture.

do

did

dog

did

dig

did

do

did

do

did

23

Trace.

Find each **found**. Color that gift purple.
Then color the rest of the picture.

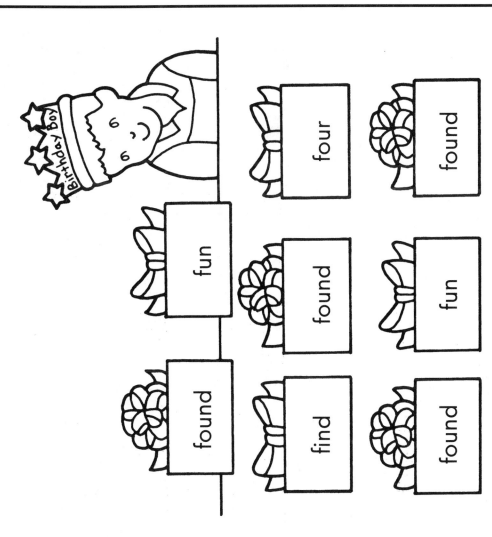

fun

found

four

found

found

find

fun

found

Write **found**.

Find each **from**. Color that penguin tan.
Then color the rest of the picture.

four	from	found	from
from	found	from	for

Name: _____

☆24☆
☆

Trace.

from
from
from

Write **from**.

Name: _____

Trace.

funny

funny

funny

Write **funny**.

_____

Find each **funny**. Color that lily pad green. Then color the rest of the picture.

funny

funny

many

four

find

funny

funny

brown

Name: _____

Trace.

gave

gave

gave

Write **gave**.

Find each **gave**. Color that mitten blue.
Then color the rest of the picture.

gave   have   gave   gate

gave   go   got   gave

Name: _____

Trace.

get

get

get

Write **get**.

_____

_____

Find each **get**. Color that ribbon blue.
Then color the rest of the picture.

get

got

get

get

tag

get

pig

get

got

Trace.

go

go

go

Write **go**.

Find each **go**. Color that space red.
Then color the rest of the picture.

off

on

at

go

to

go

go

go

go

a

go

on

to

do

Name: _____

Trace.

g o e s

g o e s

g o e s

Write **goes**.

_____

Find each **goes**. Color that space brown.
Then color the rest of the picture.

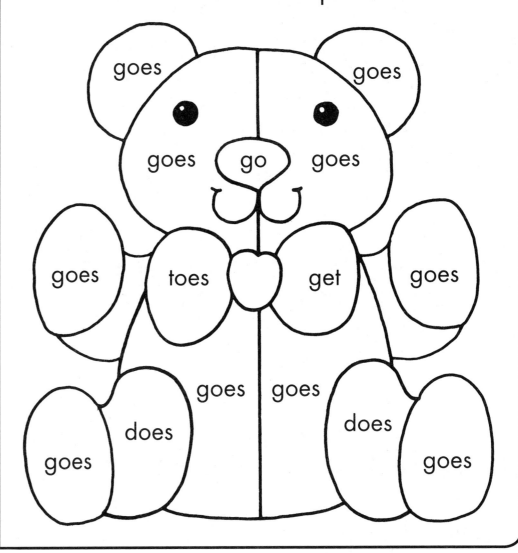

goes   goes

goes   go   goes

goes   toes   get   goes

goes   goes

goes   does   does   goes

Trace.

g o o d

g o o d

g o o d

Write **good**.

Find each **good**. Color that space pink.
Then color the rest of the picture.

good

good

good

go

dog

good

good

good

goat

Trace.

had

had

had

Write **had**.

_____

_____

Find each **had**. Color that ball yellow. Then color the rest of the picture.

dad

had

he

had

ham

add

had

had

Name: _____

Trace.

have

have

have

Write **have**.

_____

_____

Find each **have**. Color that space green.
Then color the rest of the picture.

have

have

had

have

wave

have

have

have

Trace.

h e

h e

h e

Write **he**.

Find each **he**. Color that space green. Then color the rest of the picture.

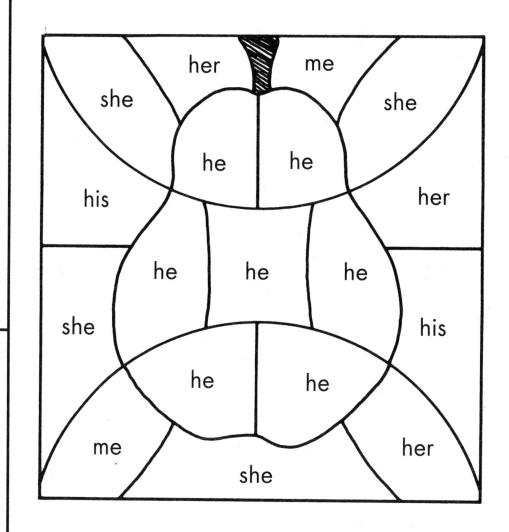

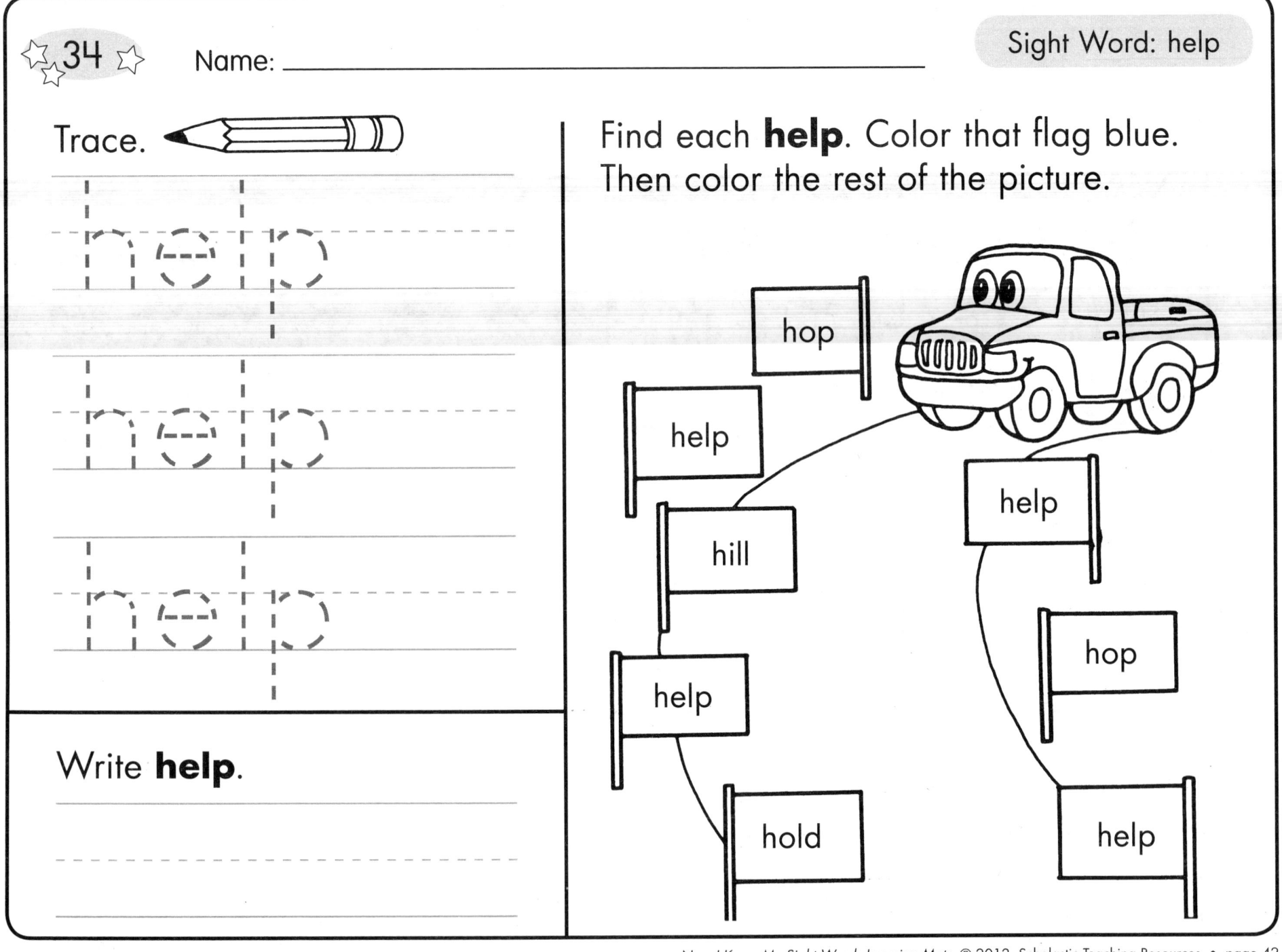

☆ 34 ☆ Name: _____

Trace.

help

help

help

Write **help**.

_____

_____

Find each **help**. Color that flag blue.
Then color the rest of the picture.

hop

help

help

hill

help

hop

hold

help

Trace.

him

him

him

Write **him**.

_____

_____

Find each **him**. Color that apple red.
Then color the rest of the picture.

hen

his

him

him

he

her

him

him

Name: _____

Trace.

his

his

his

Write **his**.

_____

_____

Find each **his**. Color that space green.
Then color the rest of the picture.

Trace.

now

now

now

Write **how**.

_____

_____

Find each **how**. Color that flower purple.
Then color the rest of the picture.

wow

now

how

how

how

how

hot

had

how

Name: _____

Trace.

i͡n͡t͡o

i͡n͡t͡o

i͡n͡t͡o

Write **into**.

_____

_____

Find each **into**. Color that train car blue.
Then color the rest of the picture.

| into | too | in |

| pin | into | fin |

| tin | into | into |

Trace.

is

is

is

Write **is**.

_____

Find each **is**. Color that space pink. Then color the rest of the picture.

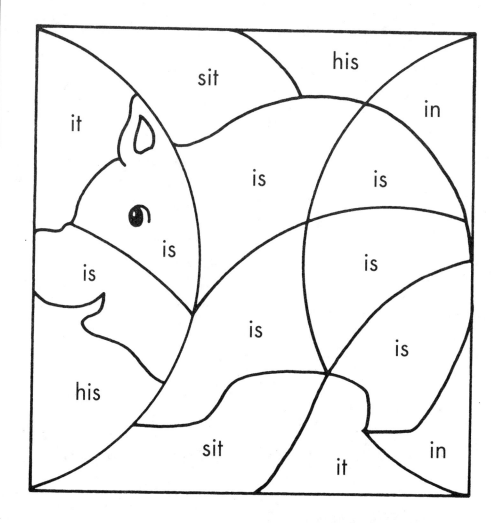

sit his

it in

is is

is

is is

is

is

his

sit in

it

☆ 42 ☆ **Name:** _____

Trace.

j u m p

j u m p

j u m p

Write jump.

_____

_____

Find each **jump**. Color that space purple. Then color the rest of the picture.

jump

pump

just

jug

jump

jam

jug

bump

just

jump

jump

Name: _____

Trace.

just

just

just

Write **just**.

_____

_____

Find each **just**. Color that book brown.
Then color the rest of the picture.

jet

just

jump

just

jug

just

jump

just

Name: _____

Trace.

like

like

like

Write **like**.

_____

Find each **like**. Color that pumpkin orange.
Then color the rest of the picture.

like

like   lid   lake

lick   like   lock   like

Trace.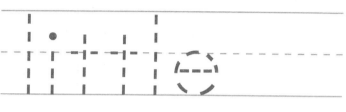

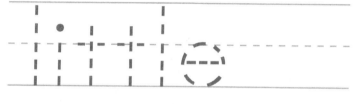

Write **little**.

_____

_ _ _ _ _ _ _ _ _ _ _ _ _

Find each **little**. Color that space black.
Then color the rest of the picture.

46 Name: ______________________

Sight Word: look

Trace.

look

look

look

Write **look**.

Find each **look**. Color that acorn brown. Then color the rest of the picture.

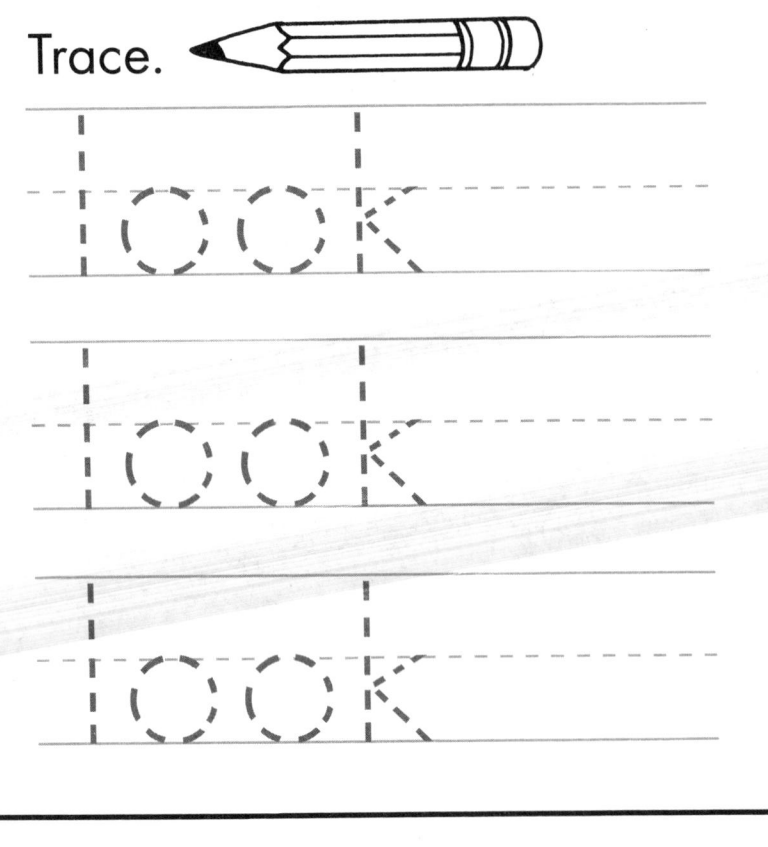

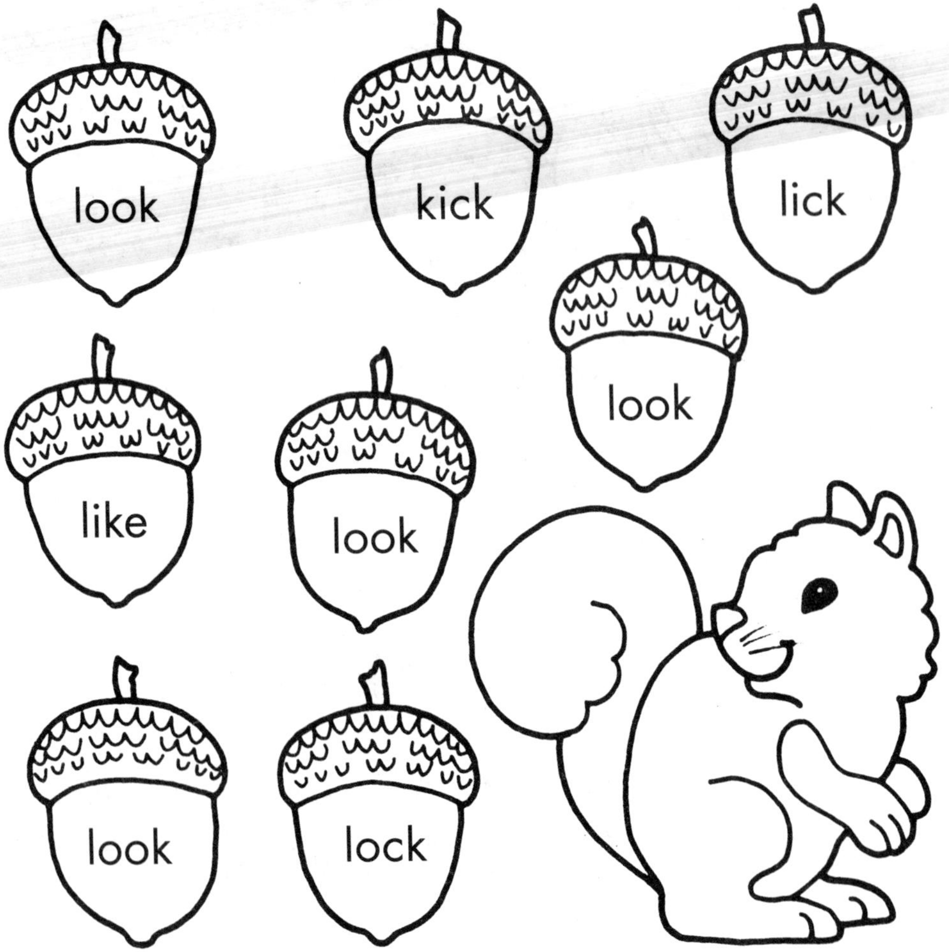

look
kick
lick
look
like
look
look
lock

Name: _____

Trace.

make

make

make

Write **make**.

_____

Find each **make**. Color that shell pink. Then color the rest of the picture.

take

make

mate

made

make

make

make

mad

Name: _____

Trace.

many

many

many

Write **many**.

_____

_____

Find each **many**. Color that cupcake yellow. Then color the rest of the picture.

many

may

man

many

many

my

any

many

Name: _____

Trace.

my

my

my

Write **my**.

_____

Find each **my**. Color that space green.
Then color the rest of the picture.

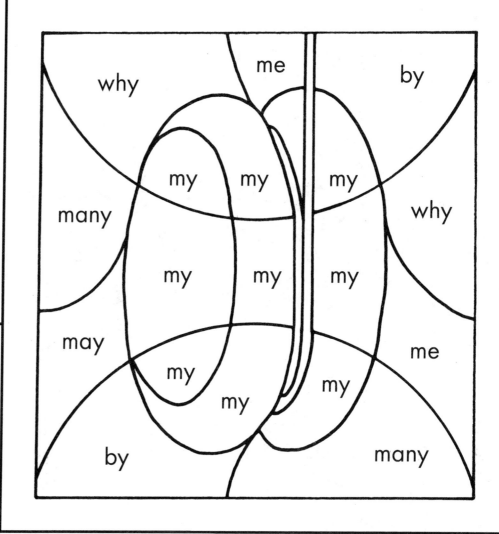

Name: _____

Trace.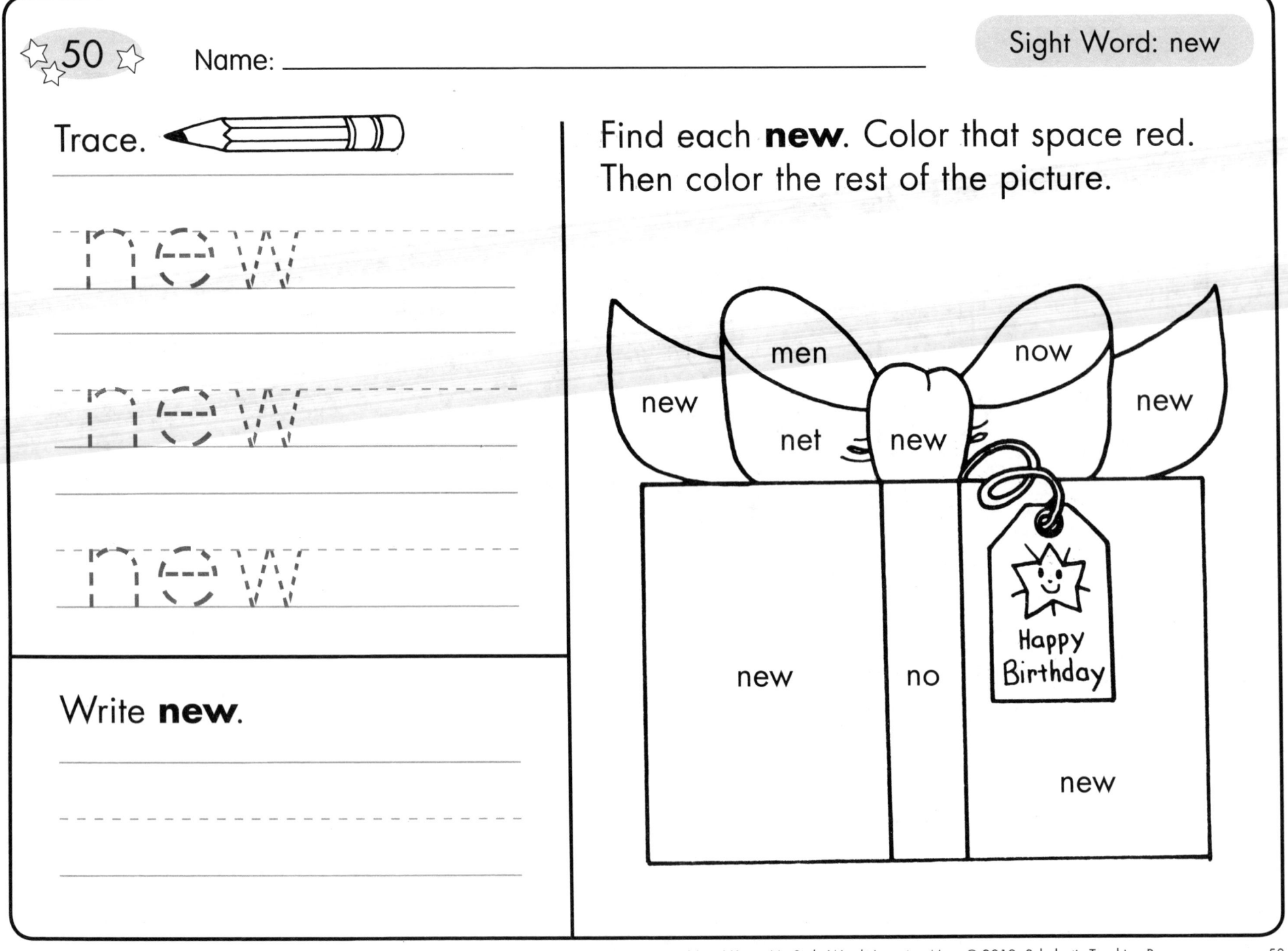

new

new

new

Write **new**.

_____

- - - - - - - - - - - - - - -

Find each **new**. Color that space red. Then color the rest of the picture.

men

now

new

new

net new

new no Happy Birthday

new

Name: _____

Trace.

no

no

no

Write **no**.

_____

Find each **no**. Color that bowling pin purple. Then color the rest of the picture.

no   now   no   not

on   no   an   no

⭐ 52 ⭐ Name: _____

Trace.

not

not

not

Write not.

_____

- - - - - - - - - - - -

Find each **not**. Color that snowflake blue. Then color the rest of the picture.

not

tan

not

not

ton

no

hot

not

Trace.

now

now

now

Write **now**.

Find each **now**. Color that space orange.
Then color the rest of the picture.

now

row

now

won

no

on

not

now

now

Trace.

of

of

of

Write of.

Find each **of**. Color that space brown.
Then color the rest of the picture.

on	of	of	an
off			for
	of	of	
out	of	of	out
	of		of
for		off	

Name: _____

Trace.

o f f

o f f

o f f

Write **off**.

- - - - - - - - - - - - - -

Find each **off**. Color that heart red.
Then color the rest of the picture.

off

of

for

off

fun

off

off

on

Name: _____

Trace.

Write **on**.

_____

Find each **on**. Color that toy blue.
Then color the rest of the picture.

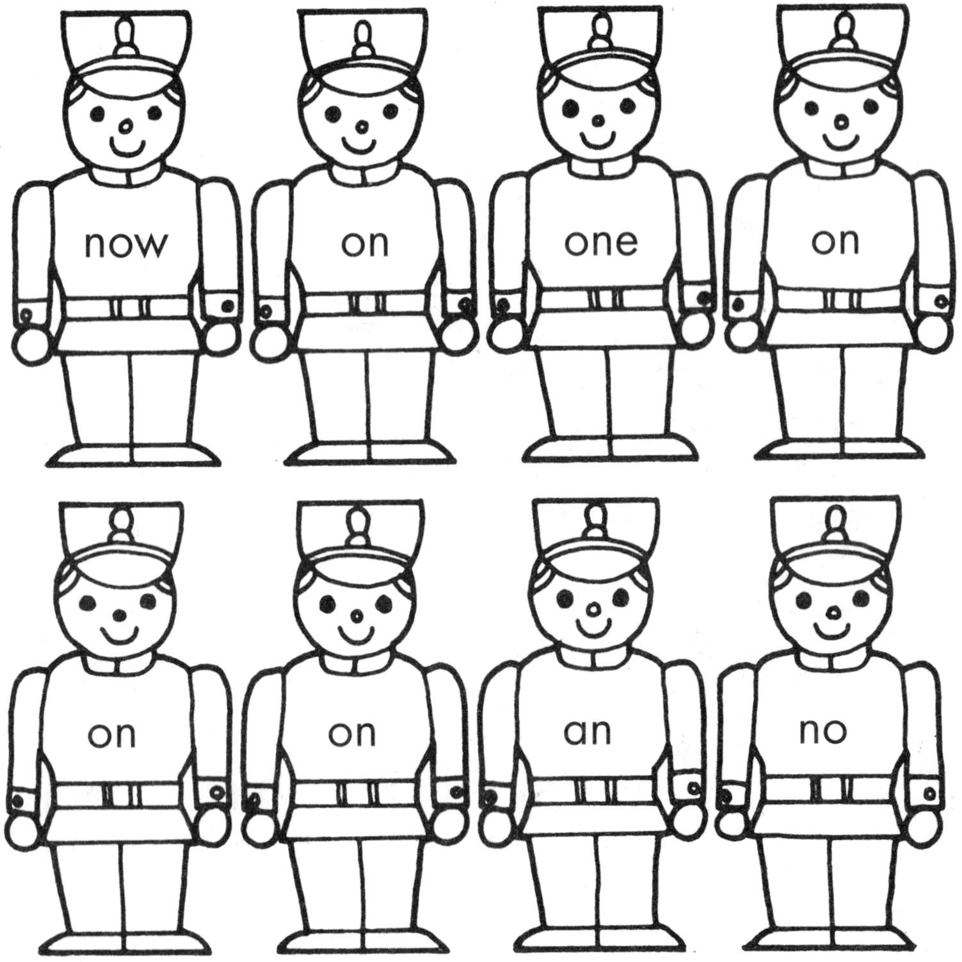

now	on	one	on
on	on	an	no

Name: _____

Trace.

our

our

our

Write **our**.

_ _ _ _ _ _ _ _ _ _ _ _ _ _ _ _ _ _

Find each **our**. Color that space black.
Then color the rest of the picture.

our

at

our

our

on

our

out

out

Name: _____

Trace.

out

out

out

Write **out**.

Find each **out**. Color that space brown.
Then color the rest of the picture.

our

out   on

of   out

out   own

our   out

out

Trace.

over

over

over

Write **over**.

Find each **over**. Color that wing gray.
Then color the rest of the picture.

over   our

out   over

over

ever

our   over

Name: _____

Trace.

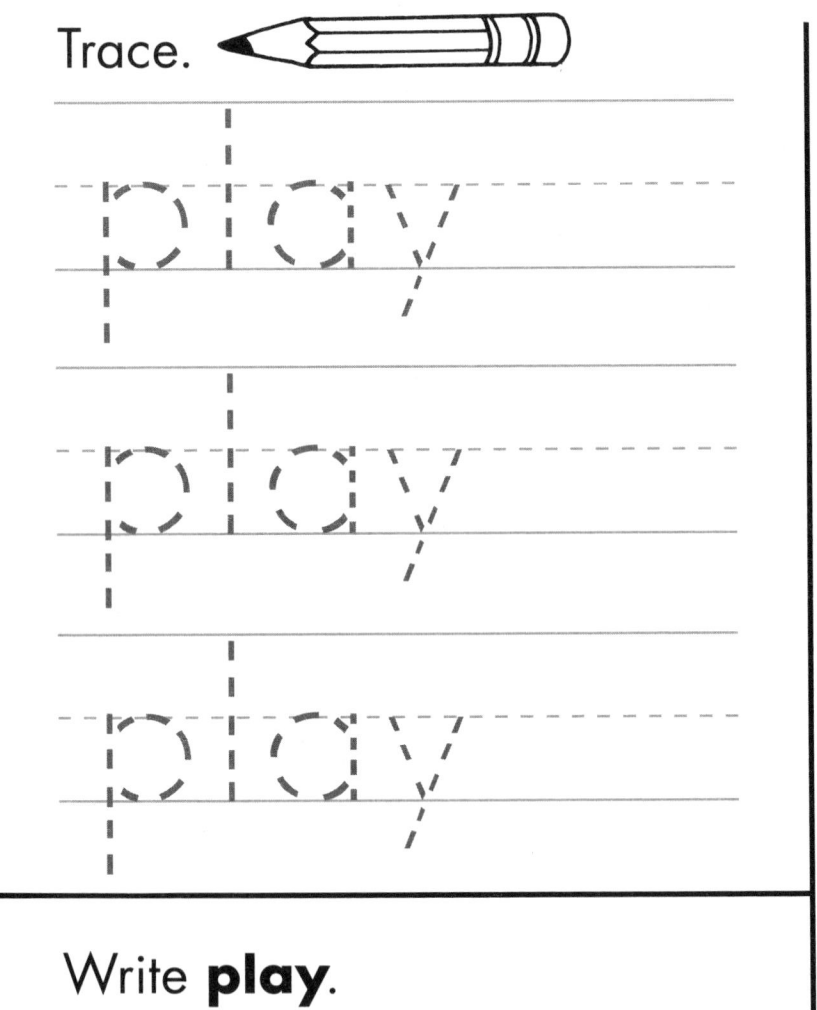

Write **play**.

Find each **play**. Color that space pink. Then color the rest of the picture.

Trace.

please

please

please

Write **please**.

_____

_____

Find each **please**. Color that space purple. Then color the rest of the picture.

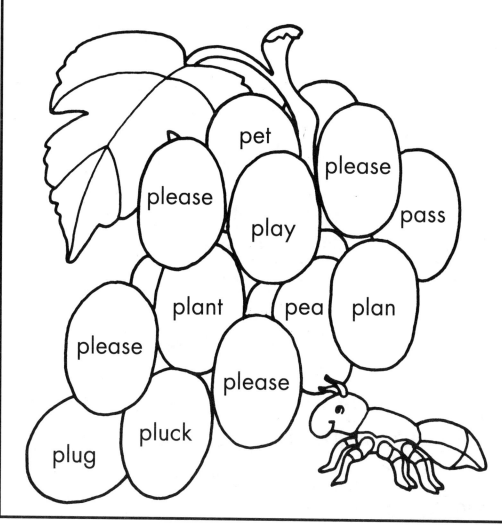

Trace.

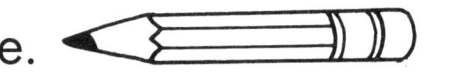

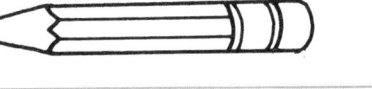

Write **pretty**.

_____

Find each **pretty**. Color that space yellow. Then color the rest of the picture.

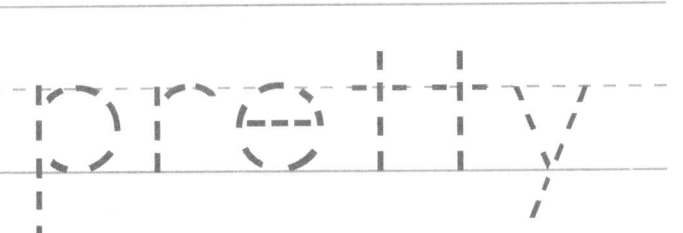

pet

pretty   pretty

pray   pretty   press   pet

pet   put

print   pretty

Trace.

put

put

put

Write **put**.

_____

_____

Find each **put**. Color that space green. Then color the rest of the picture.

put   hut   put   at

tap   put   pat   if

pet   put   put   it

Trace.

read

read

read

Write **read**.

_____

_____

Find each **read**. Color that space orange.
Then color the rest of the picture.

red

read

deer

read

read

dad

rear

read

Name: _____

Trace.

red

red

red

Write **red**.

_____

Find each **red**. Color that space red.
Then color the rest of the picture.

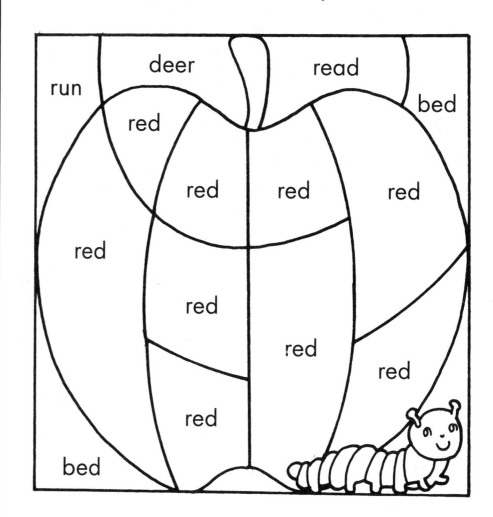

Name: _____

Trace.

ride

ride

ride

Write **ride**.

_____

_____

Find each **ride**. Color that space blue.
Then color the rest of the picture.

read

ride

ride

it

red

in

ride

rid

side

ride

rip

run

Trace. ✏️

said

said

said

Write **said**.

_____

_____

Find each **said**. Color that space brown.
Then color the rest of the picture.

Name: _____

Trace.

Write **saw**.

Find each **saw**. Color that butterfly purple. Then color the rest of the picture.

Trace.

say

say

say

Write **say**.

Find each **say**. Color that space gray. Then color the rest of the picture.

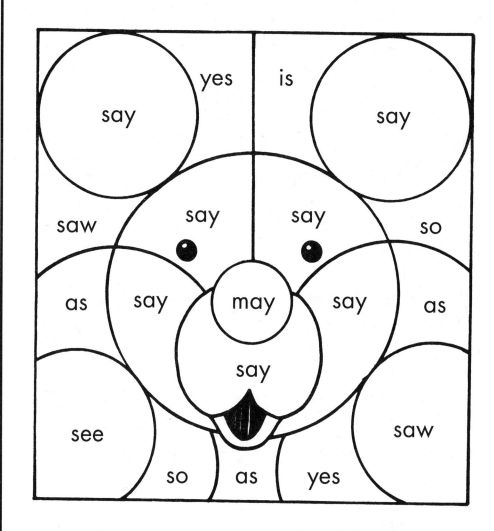

Name: _____

Trace.

s̲e̲e̲

s̲e̲e̲

s̲e̲e̲

Write **see**.

Find each **see**. Color that bee yellow. Then color the rest of the picture.

saw   see   so   see   she   seen   see   see

Trace.

she

she

she

Write **she**.

_____

_____

Find each **she**. Color that space green.
Then color the rest of the picture.

she

her   shoe

the

she

he

she

she

his

see

she

74

Name: _____

Trace.

Write **so**.

_ _ _ _ _ _ _ _ _ _ _ _ _ _ _ _

Find each **so**. Color that space yellow. Then color the rest of the picture.

Name: _____

Trace.

some

some

some

Write **some**.

Find each **some**. Color that balloon red.
Then color the rest of the picture.

Name: _____

Trace.

Write **soon**.

_____

Find each **soon**. Color that tree green.
Then color the rest of the picture.

Name: _____

Trace.

that

that

that

Write **that**.

_____

_____

Find each **that**. Color that ribbon blue. Then color the rest of the picture.

Name: _____

Trace.

the

the

the

Write **the**.

_____

_____

Find each **the**. Color that space gray.
Then color the rest of the picture.

the

then

ten

the

the

too

that

the

Name: _____

Trace.

then

then

then

Write **then**.

_____

Find each **then**. Color that strawberry red. Then color the rest of the picture.

Trace.

~~there~~

~~there~~

~~there~~

Write **there**.

_____

Find each **there**. Color that space brown.
Then color the rest of the picture.

there

them

there

the   there

then

there   their

Trace.

they

they

they

Write **they**.

Find each **they**. Color that space orange.
Then color the rest of the picture.

they

the

they

they

them

he

hay

then

they

☆84☆ Name: _____

Trace.

Write **this**.

_____

Find each **this**. Color that rocket blue.
Then color the rest of the picture.

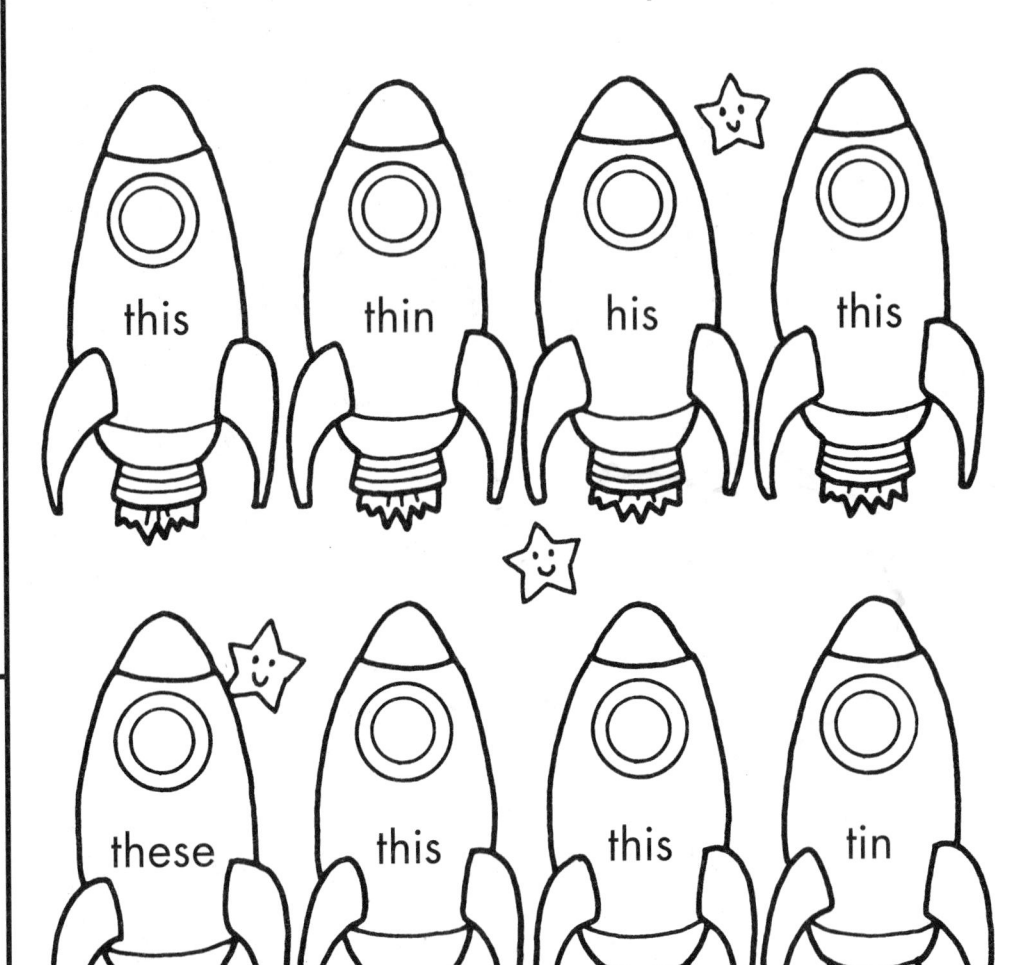

Name: _____

Trace.

too

too

too

Write **too**.

_____

Find each **too**. Color that space red.
Then color the rest of the picture.

ton

too

toe

too

out

to

too

too

☆ 86 ☆   Name: _____

Trace.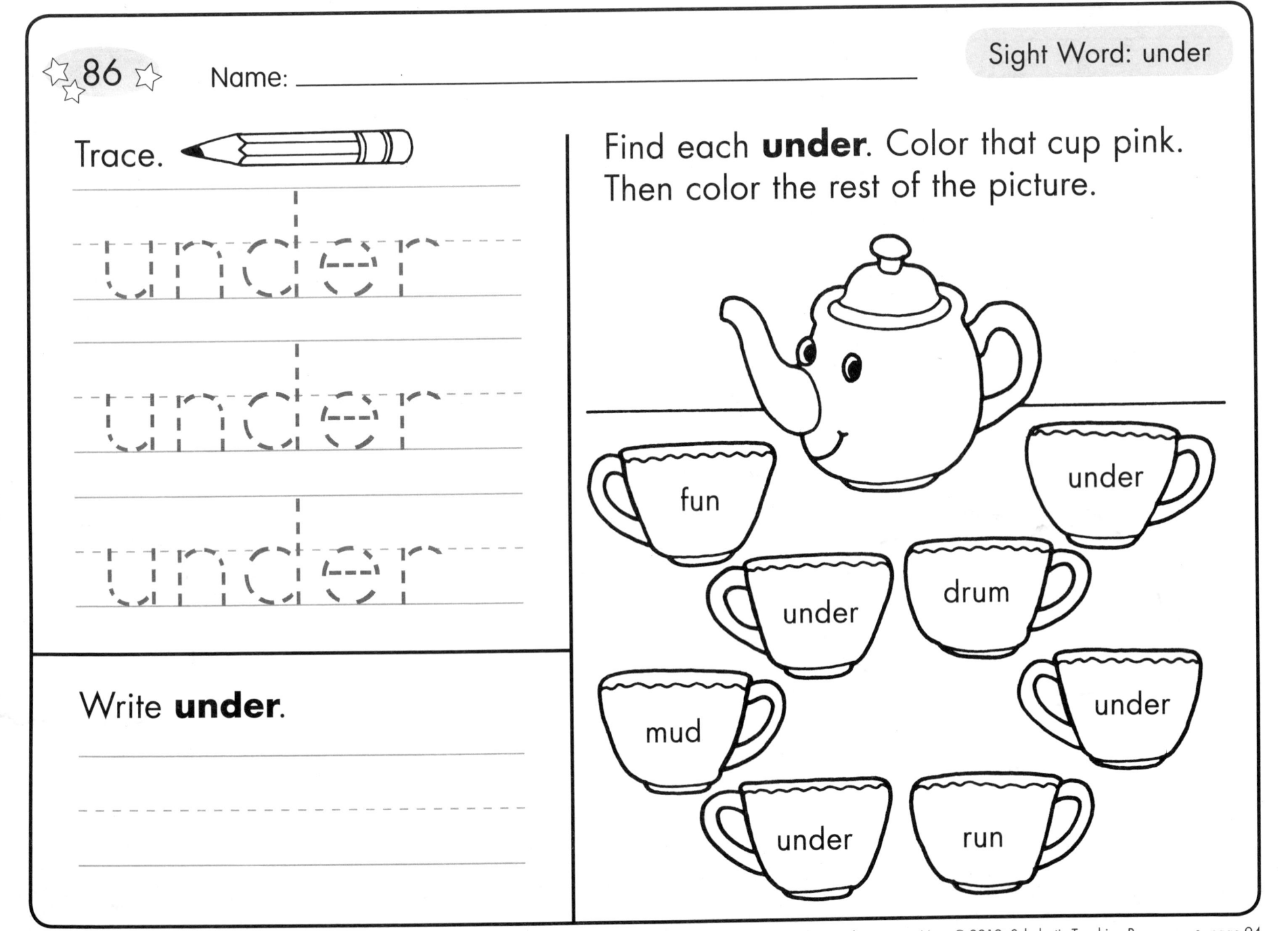

under

under

under

Write **under**.

_____

_____

Find each **under**. Color that cup pink.
Then color the rest of the picture.

fun

under

under

drum

mud

under

under

run

Name: _____

Trace.

US

US

US

Write **us**.

Find each **us**. Color that space yellow.
Then color the rest of the picture.

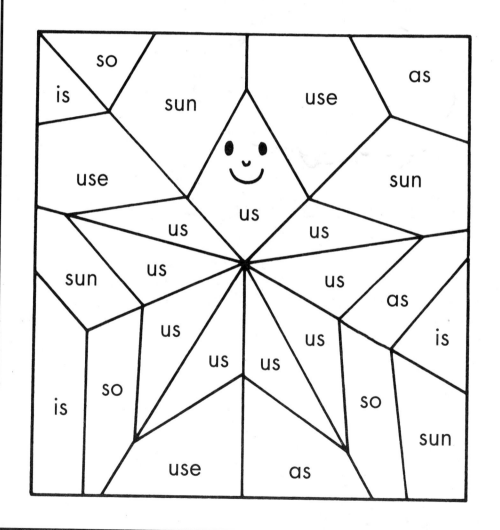

☆88☆ Name: _____

Trace.

very

very

very

Write **very**.

_____

_____

Find each **very**. Color that space black.
Then color the rest of the picture.

very   way

very   yes

very

vase   very

wave

very

Trace.

want

want

want

Write **want**.

_____

- - - - - - - - - - - - - - - - - - -

_____

Find each **want**. Color that jellybean red. Then color the rest of the picture.

want   what   want   went

was   want   want   west

Trace.

W̶a̶s̶

W̶a̶s̶

W̶a̶s̶

Write **was**.

_____

Find each **was**. Color that cracker orange. Then color the rest of the picture.

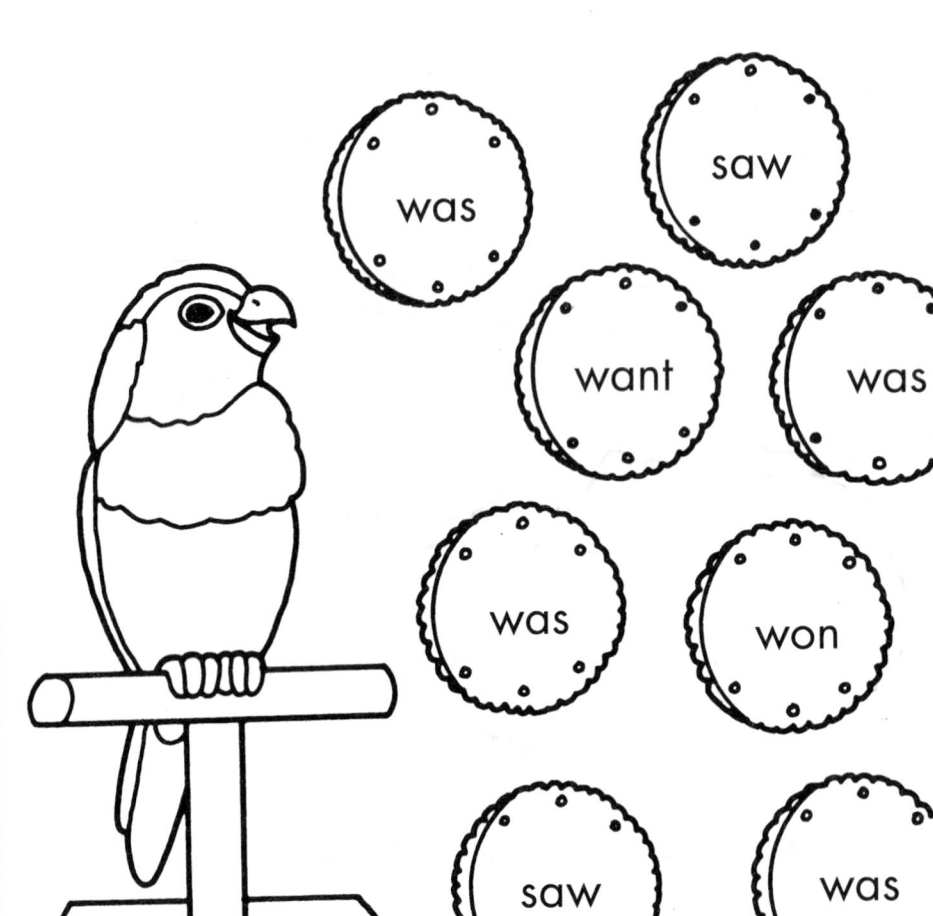

was   saw

want   was

was   won

saw   was

Trace.

well

well

well

Write **well**.

_____

Find each **well**. Color that bear brown.
Then color the rest of the picture.

wall   well   well   when

well   went   will   well

Trace.

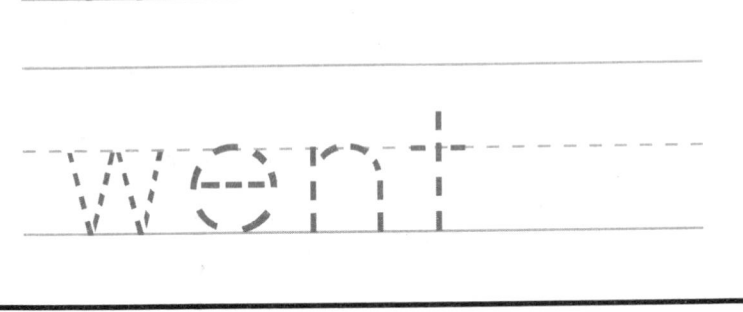

Write **went**.

_____

_____

Find each **went**. Color that pencil yellow. Then color the rest of the picture.

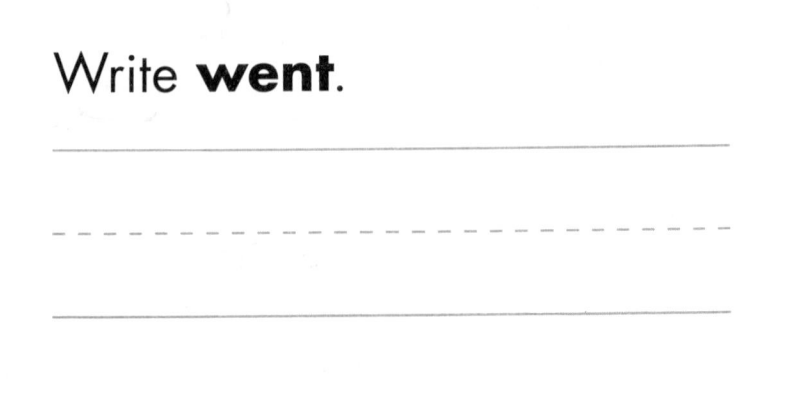

went	new
want	went
went	when
win	went

Name: _____

Trace.

were

were

were

Write **were**.

Find each **were**. Color that space blue.
Then color the rest of the picture.

were	where	were	wore
we	were	when	were

Trace.

what

what

what

Write **what**.

_____

Find each **what**. Color that ball green.
Then color the rest of the picture.

(what)   (hat)   (went)   (what)

(what)   (when)   (what)   (want)

Name: _____

Trace.

when

when

when

Write **when**.

_____

Find each **when**. Color that pie brown.
Then color the rest of the picture.

when

hen

were

when

well

when

when

went

Name: _____

Trace.

where

where

where

Write **where**.

_____

_____

Find each **where**. Color that space yellow. Then color the rest of the picture.

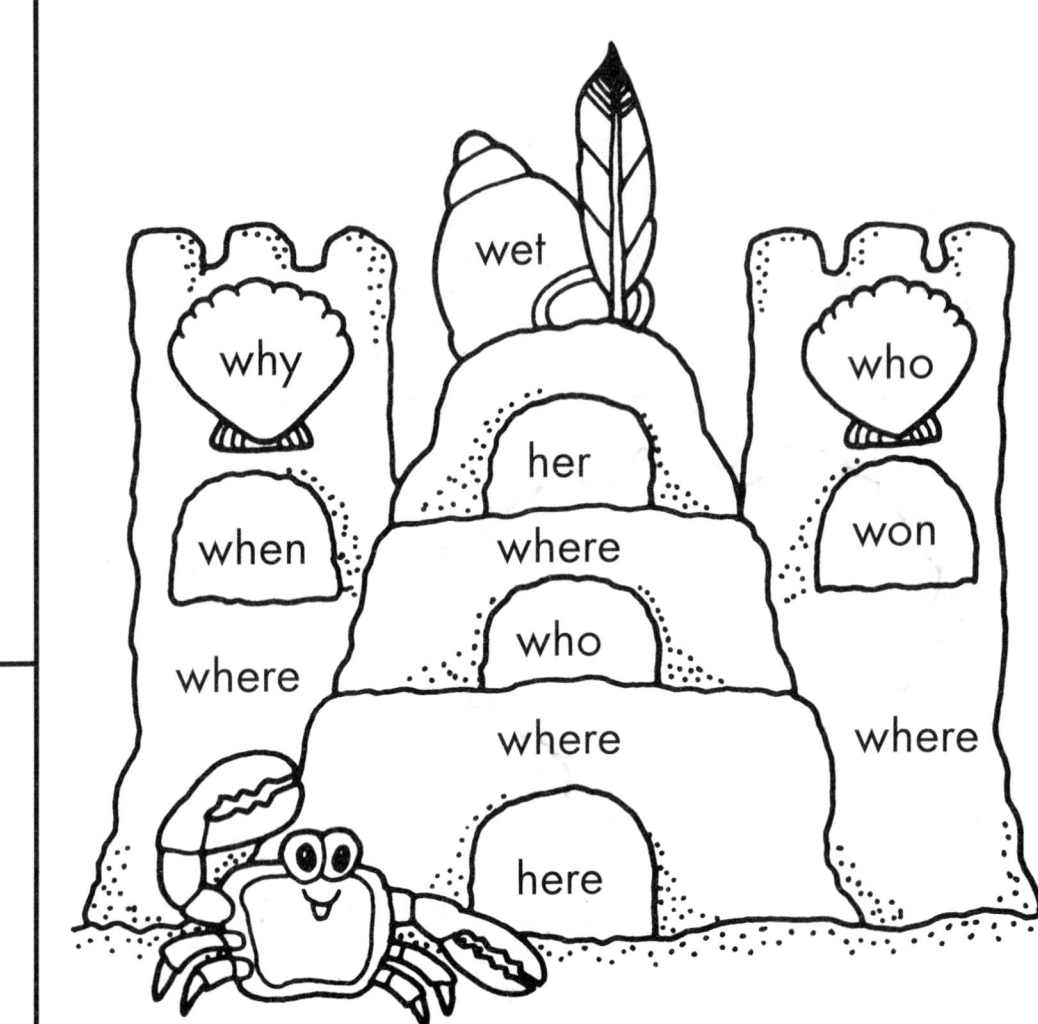

Name: _____

Trace.

who

who

who

Write **who**.

_____

- - - - - - - - - - - - - - - - -

Find each **who**. Color that space orange.
Then color the rest of the picture.

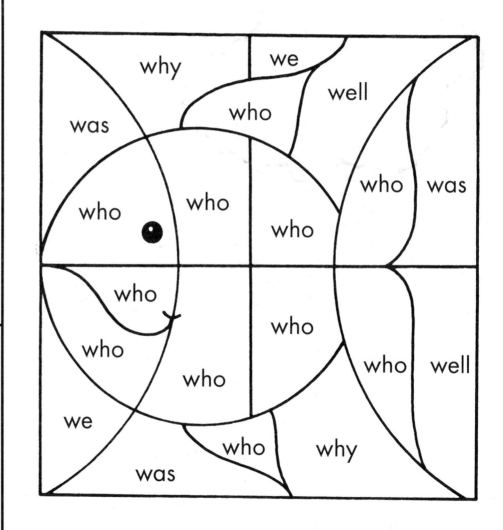

 98   Name: _____

Trace.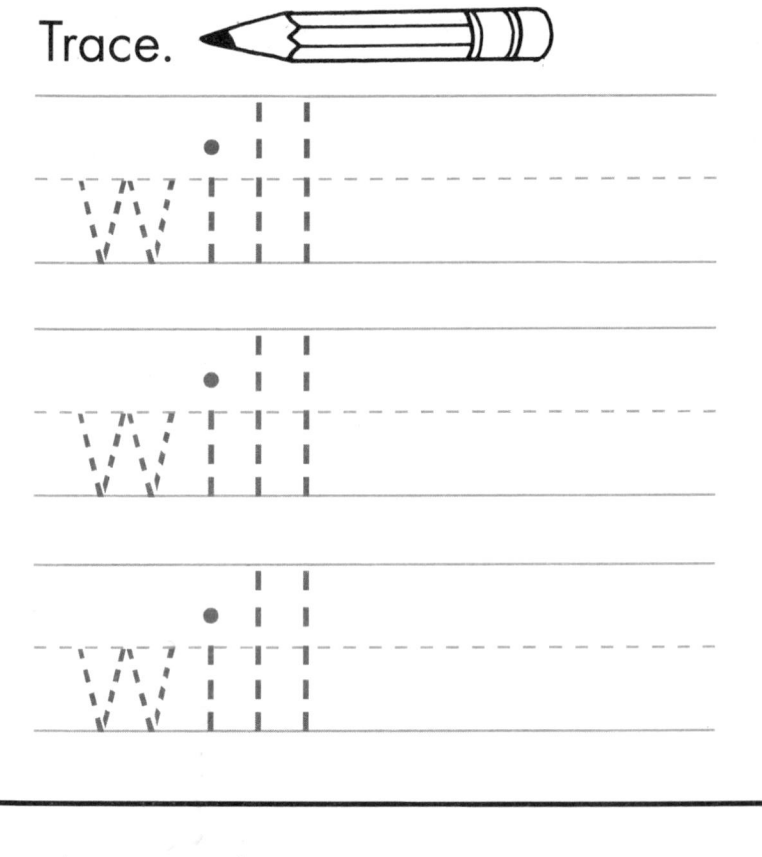

w i l l

w i l l

w i l l

Write **will**.

_____

Find each **will**. Color that float yellow.
Then color the rest of the picture.

with

will

win

will

hill

will

mill

will

Trace.

with

with

with

Write **with**.

_____

Find each **with**. Color that bag red.
Then color the rest of the picture.

with   will   with   wind

win   with   wet   with

Trace.

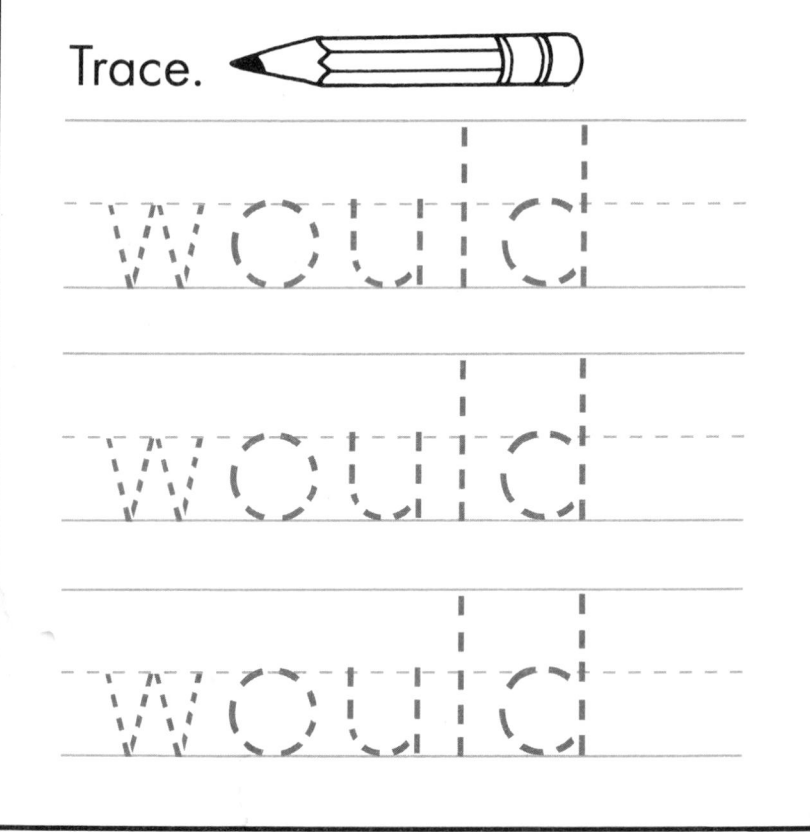

Write **would**.

Find each **would**. Color that sail purple. Then color the rest of the picture.

cold	would	could
would	down	
would	worm	would

Trace.

yellow

yellow

yellow

Write **yellow**.

_____

_____

Find each **yellow**. Color that flower yellow. Then color the rest of the picture.

yellow   yes   yellow   lily

little   yellow   yet   yellow

Name: _____

Trace.

y̶e̶s̶

y̶e̶s̶

y̶e̶s̶

Write **yes**.

_____

_ _ _ _ _ _ _ _ _ _ _ _ _

_____

Find each **yes**. Color that space orange. Then color the rest of the picture.

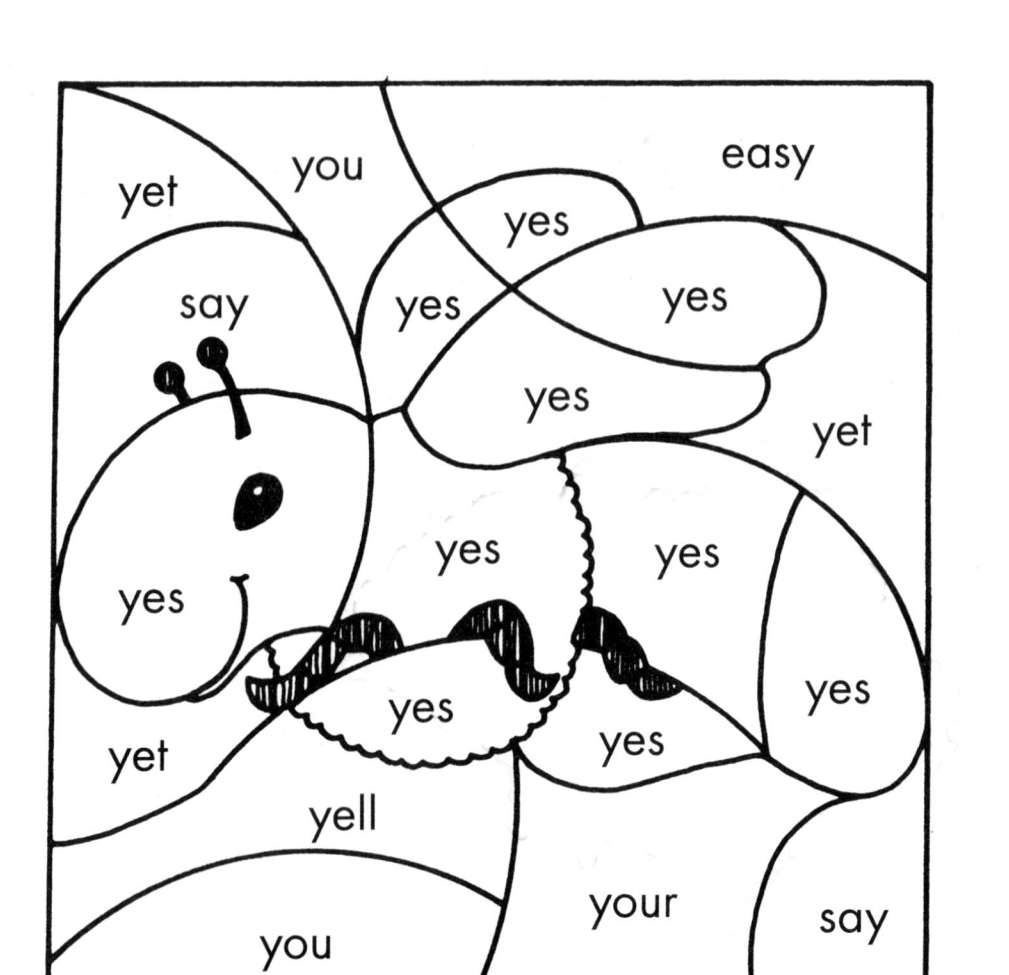

Name: _____

Trace.

you

you

you

Write **you**.

- - - - - - - -

Find each **you**. Color that egg brown.
Then color the rest of the picture.

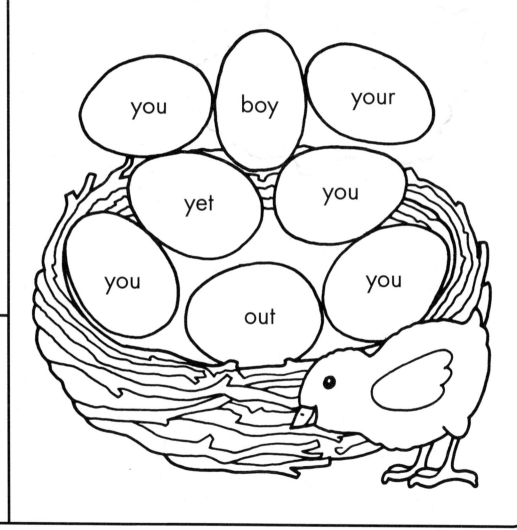

you   boy   your

yet   you

you   you

out

Trace.

your

your

your

Write **your**.

_____

_____

Find each **your**. Color that puff red.
Then color the rest of the picture.

four

your

your

your

you

our

joy

your